Butthole!

Butthole!!

Butthole!!!

A play by Wolf Larsen

Please note:

If it is not possible to have a symphony orchestra, you may substitute other instruments to accompany this play. Or you can just use some recorded music. Or you could have no music at all, but I think having music where indicated would be better. Some letters are capitalized in the middle of sentences. You can choose to ignore this, or you can choose to use this to pronounce the phrases in a 12 tone scale, as in Arnold Schoenberg. Do almost anything you want, but do not censor my play!

ABOUT WOLF LARSEN

Wolf Larsen is a comedian, writer, and poet who has traveled through over 50 countries. Wolf worked for years as a seasonal laborer in Alaska. His fiction and poetry has been published in literary magazines around the world.

Other Books by Wolf Larsen

Capitalism Sucks (non-fiction)

Honky Fucking Crazy N-Word Lover (a novel)

Pricks, Cunts, & Motherfuckers: The Novel About New York City

Eulogy for the Human Race (poems)

Pornography (poems)

Penis! Penis!! Penis!!! (a play)

Ten Thousand Penises in Your Ear (a novel)

There are many other books by Wolf Larsen to choose from. Most of Wolf's books can be purchased at online retailers.

5

Butthole! Butthole!! Butthole!!!

A play by Wolf Larsen

The first man: "I See so many faces in a sea of space alien gook! What audience of Jack-o'-lanterns from a bunch of horny mothers is this?"

The second man: "You know that tornadoes & skyscrapers taste good with lots of jizz! So, how you gonna conquer eternity in this play?"

The first man: "Don't Masturbate with me! You know My horoscope!"

The second man: "Know what bugs me so much? That Psycho in the White House! It's always some psycho in the White House, regardless of that

Demopublican or Republicrap stuff! You vote?"

The first man: "No! You the one that's Dancing with those wolves on your roof at night! You might as well Masturbate with King Kong!"

The second man: "I might as well Masturbate with King Kong? What kind of Outer space is that?"

The first man: "It's boogers in your Nuclear war Salad, that's what it is! You got a problem With that? Then you can eat lots of deranged things!"

The second man: "Yes! Yes to Boogers in your Syphilis salad! Can't you see the Armies of Silly staring at us?"

The first man: "All I see is a bunch of Faces! So you can go Take a hike to The interior of somebody else's mind!"

The second man: "Me? What about you? You the one that's always Sticking your tongue up Mother Teresa's twat!"

The first man: "At least I don't be Attacking the passerby with my penis launcher! You ain't nothing but Trouble! You the kind of trouble that Ends up in jail every weekend!"

The second man: "So much Octopus Pussy! You too much jumping & jumping & jumping! And you Always be eating them space stations out of the toilet! So go pontificate your salami brains on that!"

The first man: "Why don't you eat that Martian-art-masterpiece with lots of doo-doo? Why don't you go eat some nostalgia?"

The second man: "Why don't YOU go Eat some nostalgia?"

10

The first man: "Me go what? What kind of Space station of lunatics is this? Everybody might as well be Lost in some lunatic's dungeon! I can't stand flying around this Circus anymore!"

The second man: "I can't stand it either! It's all a bunch of Eggs falling from outer space! And when That kosher pussy ain't on the planet of impossible things, then it's tooty fruits!"

The first man: "My Pussy is A gift from God! I think it's time for Jumping in a time machine!"

The violin plays some tiMe-maChiNe-fUn...

The second man: "But what Bucket full of logic is this?"

The first man: "I don't know. I think it's Nuclear war. But maybe it's some Alfred E Newman Penis to eat."

The clarinet plays a Buffet of Alfred E Newman Penis...

The second man: "But, what about the Radio playing lots of Elephant cum?"

The first man: "Sometimes, but then other times, it's A bunch of circus clown politicians all screaming out of your radio. So much Looney Tunes political insane asylum blaring from Washington DC!"

The second man: "So much Insane self-portraits painted by all the children in your testicles?"

The first man: "Yeah! Because of the weather! With this weather there's always bees flying out of everybody's buttholes!"

The second man: "But everybody's against the weather. So we have to Invent some weather for ourselves!"

The cello plays Everybody inventing lots of weather...

The first man: "WOW! That's Some psychedelic weather! I hope it doesn't cause my brains to go thundering & lightning!"

The second man: "Well, the writer Of this here play is Vacationing in The mind of somebody in the audience."

The first man: "What about the audience?"

The second man: "What about them?"

All the violins play Thunderstorms in the insane asylum...

The first man: "But then there's the Psycho killer children of Other planets!"

The second man: "There is the what?"

The first man: "Look! It's all about the journey to Everything impossible! And then you have to Dis-arrange your life into a shattering-jigsaw-puzzle! Otherwise, All these ghosts in the walls are writing symphonies! You see?"

The second man: "I see a Big testicle on the horizon! I see a big Hallucination! And I see a big Pair of tits on your mother this Christmas!"

The piano plays a Big pair of tits for Christmas. The violin plays a big Big hairy Pussy. The clarinet plays a big Fish.

The first man: "What constant up-&-down is everything?"

14

The second man: "No! No! No! It's an obscene everything! With lots of internal organs from famous people that are delicious to be eaten!"

The first man: "With lots of Delicious? Why?"

The second man: "Why not? Why not drive to hell Boiling all around you? Why not Have sex with a thousand meowing cats? Why not Juggle a bunch of Silly everything in your hands?"

The piano plays lots of why not – why not – why not?

The first man: "You see? You see the Musical notes raining out of the Madman's mind?"

The second man: "Yes! Yes to an Eternal journey into the madman's mind!"

The first man: "Do you understand all
The itchy-itchy-bedbugs screaming out of
the endless eternity of night?"

The second man: "Never mind all that
Brains going moldy! What we need is a
bunch of Madmen jumping out of
everybody's minds! And then we can
dress in metal and dance in
thunderstorms!"

The first man: "But without The nuclear
missile launch codes, how can we Enjoy
our hamburgers?"

The second man: "You're getting lost in
the Thunderstorm! You need a mermaid
from one of Dr. Seuss's books to save
you!"

The first man: "To save me? I need to be
saved from God's lightning! And you
need to be saved from Your mother's
words boiling & boiling all around you!"

The second man: "Don't tell me what I need to be saved from! I know my own Doggy testicles!"

The violins all start playing Doggy testicles on a sunny day in the park. The woodwinds are all playing The playwright's corpse hanging from the ceiling going back-&-forth. The brass section is playing The reader being transported to the land of fire & crazy. And it all sounds like Your entire family dying in front of your eyes...

The second man: "STOP! Stop the sanity issuing forth from all those crazy rocket ships in everybody's testicles!"

(The music stops.)

The first man: "I thought we were going to Hell."

The second man: "Well, I thought we were going to Heaven."

The first man: "It must be a confusion of Which doorbell to ring, or whose Cock to suck."

The second man: "No, it's a confusion of Musical-Chair-Russian-Roulette!"

The entire symphony orchestra plays cOnFuSioN-coNfUsiOn-cOnFuSioN...

The first man: "Well, what's the Stock options on that musical-chair Russian-roulette?"

The second man: "It has something to do with Your mother riding that nuclear missile all the way to Your childhood."

The first man: "Really? But how about Those cornfields growing in your mama's Pussy?"

The second man: "Interstate commerce to that! How about a field of Penises growing across the floors of all the libraries?"

The first man: "But then Magical Balloons will happen!"

The second man: "No it won't! Everything on the planet will grow two legs and march back-&-forth like Military parades of wild animals on crack-cocaine!"

The entire symphony orchestra plays eVeRyThiNg-evErYtHinG-eVerYtHiNg...

The first man: "What we need is some Orangutans & giraffes & dairy cows all dancing the Presidential elections here on stage!"

The second man: "Absolutely not! That would cause The stock market to crash!"

The first man: "That's only because Your mother has a cornfield growing in her Vagina!"

The second man: "No! It's because of the Spanish Inquisition!"

The first man: "You Lost on somebody else's planet?"

The second man: "No, you lost in All kinds of crazy outer space!"

The first man: "How? With all this Penis music how can anybody lose?"

The second man: "You can Stick your penis into a Hyper-Mania-Machine!"

The first man: "I find that to be so gobbledygook that I vomit all my hysteria at you! Especially with all the people being stolen!"

The second man: "Well then you can Go find yourself some other planet Earth to live on!"

The first man: "Without a Penis?"

The piano begins playing a waltz of decapitated bodies dancing around the planet Mars...

A woman walks on stage.

The woman says: "I would like to introduce myself to all the Mass shooters In the audience!"

And then the woman begins dancing. As the Violin plays Mass shooters having a holiday in your attic, the woman dances Like orangutans & giraffes & dairy cows all dancing together...

The first man says: "I think I found the love of my life in a nest full of question marks & exclamation points!"

And then the first man begins dancing
like all the incest in the Old Testament,
as the second violin plays a drug trip
flying down & down into the bottom of
humanity's soul...

The second man says: "All the subway
trains in New York City are really space
alien spermatozoa! All the subway
tunnels in New York City are really space
alien Vaginas!"

And as the second man begins dancing
like Emerging Dawn fucking the night sky
up the ass, the third violin plays God
peeing on this play.

And the woman says: "I lost my virginity
to an ancient Egyptian goddess in a
Toilet stall in a truck stop!"

And the woman dances like Stalinism on
the moon, and the first violin plays like
Thousands of amputated penises...

And the first man says: "I keep throwing up Lots of art Out of my lungs every day!"

And as the first man dances Like happy-happy-deodorant-commercials on television, the second violin plays Rats & cockroaches dancing together in the playwright's kitchen...

And the second man says: "It's time for Lots of insects eating through your minds!"

And as the second man dances like Your mother, the violin plays The Devil painting a canvas of the sins of evil conquering the world...

And then the entire symphony Orchestra plays a bunch Of Siamese twins having heart attacks. And then the entire orchestra plays The sunshine having a nervous breakdown. And then the entire orchestra plays Friday making love to Thursday morning...

And then silence...

The first man: "My boogers are for sale on the Internet!"

The woman: "That's very Freudian with lots of Pussy juices!"

The second man: "You should Give a speech about Freud's butthole to all the Vaginas at the edge of your sanity!"

The woodwinds all play a bunch of Wild lions & tigers devouring the audience...

The first man makes cOuNtrY-weSteRn-diScO-dAnCiNg movements as he says: "I would like to invite the entire audience to my studio apartment this evening, so that we can all travel to an afternoon that happened 1,000 years ago together!"

The woman Dances like a bunch of animals escaping from the zoo as she says: "My boyfriend and I used to fornicate lots of riOts-iN-tHe-sTreeTs together. But then we started writing all kinds of Fantasies all over each other's naked bodies. We found this to be much more Volcanoes with whipped cream."

The second man makes Choo-choo train movements as he yells: "This theater is about to be eaten by the playwright's mother! You all better Hide in each other's booty holes!"

The brass section all plays a bunch of Choo-choo Trains going wild...

The woman screeches: "I want All the choo-choo trains in my brains to take me to Paradise! I want the paradise where the run-on sentences are running amok and having orgies with each other!"

The second man moves like The avant-garde meets a drive-by shooting...

The first man screeches: "I want my dizzy dreams! I want everybody's dizzy dreams! But with lots of pee dripping all over everybody's dreams!"

The woman moves like Cheese on asparagus...

The second man screeches: "I want my Homicides with lots of fresh cherries!"

And then all the violins together start playing Homicide on a beautiful sunny day...

And then, as the flute plays A man jumping from a tall building, and the woman dances like Indian summer coming to an end, the first man says: "Let's All jump into each other's heads! Too much fried Artist in the pan for me to bear! Let's Christmas together with lots of Saturn's rings rolling around us!"

And then, as the oboe plays Lots of pornography, the first man dances like Masturbating supernovas, as the second man says: "Chopping up Albert Einstein into pieces and eating him is the answer! No! Having sex with a thousand Santa Clauses is the answer! Does anybody have my childhood?"

And then, as the flute plays Jesus Christ masturbating, the second man dances like Choo-choo trains floating off the planet Earth, as the woman says: "I lost my vagina! Where should I go? Can any of you please give me some songs about being kidnapped by a circus clown and taken to a place that doesn't exist yet?"

And then the piano plays some fast-paced Oral sex as both men & women dance like Igor Stravinsky running from 10,000 horny space aliens...

And then all is silent. Nobody is moving...

The woman whispers: "I have All 535 congressmen on Capitol Hill in my Vagina!"

The first man whispers: "I think I'm having a nervous breakdown!"

The second man whispers: "That's good! Maybe you can Take a jackhammer to my brains!"

Then the woman screams: "I think I forgot my child in the Subway station!"

And then the piano plays a bunch of screaming Space aliens. And the violins Start playing a bunch of screaming dolls. And the brass section start playing a bunch of screaming Poets...

And then the woman & two men whisper together: "All the poets of the world are screaming because All the words in all the languages have disappeared!"

The flute plays a Whispering Fish...

And the woman whispers: "Tomorrow we will Hijack the entire planet Earth!"

And the oboe plays a whispering Tomorrow...

And then the second man screams: "We're all going to die from Too much happiness! It's all in the Bible! Watch out for the Frogs in your stomach!"

And then there is silence...

And in silence the two men & the woman dance a Homicidal waltz. They dance a French cooking lesson. And they dance whatever-the-craziness-that's-in-their-hearts...

And then they stop dancing.

The woman: "I've been to the Paris, France that's in my alleyway here in Idaho. But I haven't been to That planet where thoughts are bigger than the universe. Hey audience! Have you been to The alleyway behind my house? There's all kinds of ogres & hunchbacks there!"

The first man screams: "I've been to so much crazy!"

The second man whispers: "It's all A computer program that's turning us all into fried salami on an extraterrestrial sidewalk."

The woman sings: "It's all a bunch of madmen running through the mountains & valleys of your brains! It's all A bunch of insomniac salad! It's all a bunch of space aliens inside your guts!"

And as the woman & the first man watch, the second man dances in silence like a Fish changing into a human... He dances in silence like a fish on another planet... He dances in silence like a Lion being eaten alive by an ant.

Then the entire orchestra plays a Mass shooting waltz together. Then It's silent. Then the trumpet announces a great Exodus of people from their own brains...

A transsexual dances comically onto the stage. He shouts with much amusement: "I'm here to Help you all find your clones! They must be around here somewhere!"

Immediately, the two men begin sucking the cock of the transsexual, as the woman says: "The children are tomorrow's serial killers. My husband is so extraterrestrial that he kisses all the planets every night. I wonder if he suspects that the kids are not his?"

And then, as the two men suck his Kock, the transsexual says: "I like my hamburgers with lots of intergalactic invasions! I like my happiness with lots of human blood splattered everywhere! Lots of Charles Manson to you all!

And then the woodwinds do a march to a place where everything's crazy, while the brass section does a falling airplane with a CRASH, and the conga drums do lots of sex with wild animals...

And then the transsexual sings: "I lost my brains! Have you seen my brains?! I'm just a frog looking for billions of lips to kiss my derrière! And Jesus Christ & Santa Claus having sex by the Christmas tree is so achooooooooooooooo!"

And as the two men continue sucking the transsexual's Kok, the transsexual & the woman have a conversation.

The woman says: "So, how was your trip to Butthole Land?"

The transsexual says: "It was very exploding grenade, with lots of voices in everybody's heads."

The woman: "I hear that's quite Exciting if you're a Crazy man inside a ghoulish cartoon that you can't escape from."

The transsexual: "No, not really, it's actually quite Like a giant castration ceremony."

The woman: "Really?"

The transsexual: "You gotta see the sexy nuns of God's harem in heaven! Let's do the Catholic cunnilingus ceremonies together!"

Then the timpani drums begin playing
Eating ice cream during a nuclear war.
And all the presidents of the United
States of America rush on stage, and
begin performing oral sex on each
other...

The transsexual sings: "The music of
Stocktonhousen saves us with so much
Electric Chairs walking everywhere!
Elliott Carter has so much Emotional
tornado to say! But I love the Bash-
everything-into-pieces of Bartok!"

The woman sings: "Let's kiss lots of
nowhere! Let's have sex with Abstract
art! There is no turning back from having
anal sex with a thousand clones of
Michelangelo's David!"

A transsexual George Washington says:
"I was a Four-star General in the
Pedophile Brigades once!"

The flute plays The Pedophile Brigades jumping out of your soup...

A transsexual Abraham Lincoln says: "Let's party! Let's party with lots of Rainbows & cocaine & castrated midgets!"

The clarinet plays a party in outer space...

A transsexual John F. Kennedy says: "I want you all to share your wives with me!"

The vibes play a wife-sharing party...

Then all the presidents have orgasms in each other's mouths as the entire symphony plays oRgaSmS-orGasMs-oRgaSmS.

Then the transsexual has orgasms in the mouths of the two men, as the entire symphony plays Transsexual Opera on the moon.

Then all the Presidents disappear as the entire symphony plays The blue sky hopping from planet to planet...

The first man says: "Oh, I wish you would ride that Tyrannosaurus rex into the Italian Renaissance!"

The second man says: "Shaking booty to that!"

The first man: "It's a holiday in Hitler's testicles!"

The second man: "It's a frightening ghost in Joseph Stalin's testicles!"

The first man: "So many big plastic boobs to play!"

The second man: "I am dizzy with rainbows CRASHING everywhere!"

Then two armies suddenly rush on stage as they fight each other. The entire symphony is playing War with lots of Cock sucking everywhere And war with delicious tasting grenades and war with lots of bullets in our love-making! It's too much Testicle helicopters doing the Tootsie-too!

And suddenly the symphony stops playing, and The timpani drums play Empires all over the universe collapsing, and all the soldiers who were fighting each other a moment ago, are now performing anal sex on each other.

The transsexual begins singing: "Everything is collapsing & falling apart! Fried onions! Give me some Penis in my mouth!"

And then the two armies of men having anal sex with each other start singing:

"We shot the generals! We shot the
dictators! We shot all the capitalist
politicians too!"

The transsexual sings: "Let me jizz all
over your patriotic values! Let's have
anal sex all over your funeral! Let's
dance the endless sweaty panties of
summer together!"

The two armies of men sing: "Anal sex
with lots of politically correct sex dolls on
the street corners! Anal sex with lots of
Hello! Lots of anal sex and more
anal sex and more anal sex!"

The transsexual sings: "Anal sex all over
the ceiling of the Sistine Chapel! Anal sex
all over the Vatican under the full moon!
Anal sex forever & ever!"

The two armies of men having anal sex
sing: "Penis lollipops for all the sunshine!
Booty holes of delight for all the Harry

Krishna-Harry Krishna-Harry Krishna!
Suck my Kock with lots of Christianity!"

And then the entire symphony orchestra
plays Cox sucking & more cock sucking &
more cock sucking, as the entire cast
dances like a cock sucking hurricane...

Then the two armies disappear.

The flute plays a Serenade for the
upcoming nuclear war.

The woman says: "Nuclear war with lots
of tomorrow."

The second man says: "I want romantic
comedy with my nuclear war."

The first man says: "Cow tits and cold
beer."

The woman says: "Little kitty cats and
Meow Meow barbecue with lots of
delicious Politicians."

The transsexual says: "A nuclear button for my dog please."

The second man says: "Let's look in the trash can, And maybe we can find some nuclear weapons."

Then the entire symphony orchestra plays An old man eating his grandson, and a donkey & an elephant walk on stage.

The donkey says: "Hi! I'm an ass!"

The clarinet laughs like an ass laughing & laughing...

The elephant says: "Hello there! I'm a rich cocaine-snorting crook that pretends to be the friend of the working class!"

The flute laughs like cocaine & more cocaine & more cocaine...

The donkey says: "I'm an ass, and I promise lots of ass for everybody!"

The clarinet laughs like a million asses all laughing & laughing.

The elephant says: "And I promise lots of Cocaine & family values! Because cocaine & family values are like twins making incest together! Cocaine & family values will make our great Nation cum all over the Virgin Mary again! Cocaine! Family values! And the red white and blue!"

The flute laughs like a laughing fiend snorting cocaine day & night & night and day & day and night...

Then a rich bourgeois pig walks on stage, as the oboe plays a funny Oink-Oink-Oink...

The rich bourgeois pig is throwing money at both the donkey & the elephant, as the entire symphony orchestra plays a funny Disaster.

Then the bourgeois pig, donkey, & elephant exit the stage, as the symphony orchestra plays a funny Whatchamacallit.

And now the transsexual begins painting all the walls of the auditorium. He's painting a bizarre Collage-of-feelings, as the flute plays Your head hemorrhaging with Art.

As the transsexual paints & the flute plays the woman says: "It's your brains bouncing across the Landscape of a madman & a genius having anal sex of the brains together! It's all a massacre of everything peaceful & quiet! It's Adolf Hitler having anal sex with a dozen black guys!"

Then the woman joins the transsexual in painting this huge painting all over the walls of the auditorium.

The first man dances to the flute going to Antarctica & the North Pole & back, while the second man says: "I lost my sanity somewhere in this play. Or did I lose my sanity in the insane asylum?"

Then the second man joins the woman & transsexual in painting the auditorium.

The first man stands on stage alone and announces: "The sunlight infects me with chainsaw massacre desires! We're all infected with the 21st Century! So let's all become bugs and fly away!"

Then the brass section plays an energetic 1950s – while everybody runs around the stage – while a narrator walks on stage and announces: "And now we're going to lots and lots of crazy bananas screaming incessantly at us at midnight! And then we're going to Eat the piano!

And then we're going to drink all the poetry out of the libraries!"

The narrator starts dancing as the transsexual speaks: "Never mind all that! Instead, we're going to paint all the music pink & yellow & light blue! And then we're going to listen to the dandelions whisper to us all night!"

Then the narrator walks offstage.

The lady says: "It's all nuclear missiles flying out of our food!"

The first man asks: "Why do you think that our food tastes like circus clowns?"

The second man asks: "Or does it have more to do with all the Orgies of Amoebas in the air?"

The transsexual asks: "Really! With all the transsexual voices in our breakfast cereal?"

The lady asks: "What diarrhea all over the walls are you talking about?"

The transsexual asks: "Is this a mathematical equation where nuclear war minus lemon meringue pie equals a big pair of buttocks?"

The second man asks: "Derangement? A brain full of Feral cats all fornicating loudly 24 hours a day? A world full of Wild-irrational-thoughts screaming loudly from every face?"

The lady asks: "Why is this So giant toilet brains in the Auditorium? Where is the Rain that will make the Erotic poetry grow? And when is the Symphony of Heart Attacks arriving?"

The transsexual asks: "How long until the the zoo of this world we live in Explodes? What's up with this man that keeps falling out of his own head? And how can we tiptoe out of this Haunted attic full of everybody's rabies?"

Then the entire orchestra plays a romantic Knife stabbing, while a bunch of male ballet dancers descend on the stage. All the male ballet dancers dance together as couples.

The lady says: "I have to fly away from here on a magical toilet!"

All the male ballet dancers shout: "Right now! Right now!"

The lady says: "Or should I Grab my surfboard and surf on over to The next wet dream?"

All the male ballet dancers shout: "Right now! Right now!"

The lady says: "Or perhaps I should get a taste of The poetry brewing in your testicles?"

All the male ballet dancers shout: "Right now! In a jiffy!"

The transsexual says: "In a jiffy all the thousands of ladybugs will be arriving here to kiss us!"

Everybody stops and stares at the transsexual...

Then the entire orchestra plays A month of manic insomnia! And all the male ballet dancers dance off the stage...

The woman turns to the others on stage and says: "Do you feel all the genitalia communicating with each other?"

The two men & the transsexual shout: "Fuck me with a Tyrannosaurus Rex Dick! We feel the genitalia of others talking to us in forbidden languages!"

The woman says: "It's the Big Bang of all the orgasms in heaven that's messing with our ears!"

The transsexual shouts: "For sure! For sure!"

Then the two men shout together: "For sure the earthquakes that we desire! For sure the Centuries of love we feel in each tormented moment!"

Then the woman sings: "I can't hide my Pussy anymore! I can't hide all the hurricanes & volcanoes & earthquakes inside of me anymore either! I can't Keep jumping off this mountain of emotions anymore either!"

Then the transsexual sings: "She can't hide her Pussy anymore! She can't Hide all the hurricanes & volcanoes & earthquakes inside of her anymore! She can't keep jumping off this mountain of emotions anymore either!"

The two men shout together: "For sure the Automation of our desires! For sure the Warriors of the pen! For sure! For sure!"

Then the entire orchestra plays All the stars in the sky masturbating as the woman starts masturbating herself with a vibrator...

Then the woman screams: "I will masturbate until the oceans carry me away!"

Then the woman whispers: "I will masturbate until The volcano of all my desires explodes its irrational beings everywhere!"

Then the entire symphony orchestra plays 10,000 years of oral sex. And a bunch of women jump up on stage, and began performing oral sex on each other as the music plays...

The transsexual shouts over the music: "200,000 years of oral sex is so very poetic!"

And all the women giving each other oral sex shout: "Why's the clock going bop with the Killer pop-pop-pop?"

The transsexual shouts: "It's the Sexy machinery going haywire with the Sexy vowels!"

All the women shout: "What's the ding-dong of the dippy doing the Quack-quack-quack?"

The transsexual shouts: "It's a lot of Penis art Doing so much Happy things! That the psYchO-muRdeRinG-aRtisT has to Remain as calm as a Earthquake crashing about in your head!"

The women shout: "It's a lot of Earthquakes crashing around in the head of some pSyChO-mUrDeRiNg-aRtiSt? But what about the Sunrises & sunsets doing the sexy-sexy together?"

Then all is silent.

And the woman says as she waves the vibrator in her hand like a magic wand: "I'm a Vagina that Go tick-tok like a clock! And now I'm a rabbit that runs off to The slaughterhouse to be happily slaughtered! But sometimes I'm a vacuum cleaner eating up all the loose words running around here!"

Then the orchestra starts playing Virgin Mary space aliens jumping out of flying saucers. And all the women Go back to performing oral sex on each other...

The transsexual shouts: "I did it! I Sold my butthole to the homeless man on Mars for $1 million Dollars!"

The woman starts pleasuring herself with the vibrator again As she shouts: "I did it too! I Sold my Vagina to the undertaker for all the bellybuttons in the world!"

All the women giving each other oral sex shout out: "We did it! We conquered the elephants in outer space!"

The woman pleasuring herself with a vibrator says: "The future is Opening up! Because we did it! We Created a Monster that sexes us like a thousand Olympic athletes on crack-cocaine!"

The women all shout: "The past is Trampling all over the future! Because we did the Future with all of our penises & booty holes!"

The woman pleasuring herself says: "So much future to build in the past! So much anal sex parades in the future! We did it! Everything is now Running away into the past!"

Then all the women performing sex on each other suddenly reached a giant noisy climax together. And the entire Symphony orchestra is playing lots of nOisY-oRgaSmiC-cLimAxeS.

And then the transsexual shouts: "And now let's all march into the Forest of sexual sculptures!"

And then all the women leave the stage.

All is silent.

And then the two men on stage begin having anal sex with each other. The flute is playing Your mother giving birth to a thousand lions & tigers...

The first man says: "The sunset is Splashing a giant orange orgasm all over us!"

The second man says: "The sunrise is Splashing a giant orange orgasm all over us too!"

The first man: "The Rain is raining the sadness of my words all over the planet Earth!"

The second man: "The sunshine is seething & seething with so much frustration!"

The first man: "The storms are coming!"

The second man: "I'm coming! I'm coming! I'm coming!"

The first man: "Oh! Oh! Oh!"

And the entire symphony orchestra plays a Storm that goes As wild as 10,000 chainsaws flying through the air, And the orchestra plays a storm that races off into the future, and the orchestra plays a storm That is all the emotions of the playwright going millions of miles an hour...

Then all is silent.

The transsexual says: "It's the silence that says so many words! It's the silence That's killing us all! So much silence!"

The woman says: "The silence is loving me!"

The transsexual says: "We must yell a bunch of silence at each other! We must sing with so much silence! We must whisper with so much noise!"

The woman says: "Our whispers are Daggers! Our shouts are sunshine! Our songs are Made of our blood dripping down the walls!"

And the entire symphony orchestra plays a Whispering storm. A crowd of people descend on the stage. And a woman politician & a male politician walk on stage as they wave to the crowd.

Over the loudspeakers the narrator says: "And now for the great debate!"

The female politician says: "My male opponent is a Tornado that never happened! Me on the other hand, I am a Verb – a silly verb that's always acting up!"

All the women in the crowd clap.

That's when the clarinet laughs like a Sunrise & a sunset having sex with each other.

The male politician says: "My female opponent is a Book that was never opened! Me on the other hand, I am a Smiling monster that will eat you all!"

All the men in the crowd clap.

The clarinet laughs again.

The female politician says: "I stand for Birds flying around in everybody's heads! I stand for sitting down! I believe in a castrated pianist in every pot in every kitchen in the nation!"

All the women in the crowd clap.

The clarinet laughs.

The male politician says: "I believe in Skinny-dipping at the North Pole! I believe in Standing on top of the planet of Jupiter and getting drunk! I stand for Erect penises in all the music on the radio!"

All the men in the crowd clap.

The entire symphony Orchestra starts laughing like a Bunch of lOud-inSanE-aLcoHoLicS...

The female politician says: "I eat all the words in your brains! And I have so much pigeons in the park to say! And I can Masturbate the big black Dick between my legs just as good as any man!"

All the women chant: "She can masturbate the big black Dick between her legs just as good as any man! Yes she can!"

And now the flute starts laughing like a Monkey that has smoked too much marijuana...

And the male politician says: "What we need is Lots & lots of salami from the deli in our buttholes! What we need is thousands of crazy faces all bouncing towards us! And we need lots of Orgies in the churches on Sundays!"

All the men begin chanting: "Orgies in the churches on Sundays! Orgies in the churches on Sundays!"

And the piano begins laughing like a Thousand television commercials where everybody's smoking crack-cocaine...

And then a rich bourgeois pig walks up on stage and starts throwing money at the male politician & the female politician as everybody claps. The orchestra starts playing a Beat-yOur-kiDs-Kind-Of-waltZ. And now all the people & the two politicians & the rich bourgeois pig walk offstage...

The transsexual says: "I believe in Throwing All my thoughts into the seas of transsexual cum!"

The woman says: "What we need is More orangutans & chimpanzees & monkeys in this play! You can never have enough orangutans & chimpanzees & monkeys in a play!"

The first man says: "Lots of 1970s to all that! Let's have sex with all the orangutans & chimpanzees & monkeys! Let's all go with the audience to the zoo!"

The second man says: "Smash everything into pieces with a baseball bat! Masturbate to everything! Let's have sex with the sun & the moon & all the planets! Let's all go into outer space with the audience!"

Then the narrator says over the loudspeaker: "Okay audience! Now it's time for endless talking toilets all talking at once!"

Then the entire symphony orchestra plays a Crack-smoking Star-Spangled Banner. A whole bunch of people walk on stage, Including a white & a black politician waving to their supporters.

The white politician says: "We believe in riding horny zebras to all the orgies of the Kings & Queens of Mars! We need more holes in the universe to jump into! The problem with this country is too much Kalamazoo, Michigan in all of our dog's buttholes!"

All the white people on stage yell: "Too much dog's buttholes talking to us out of politician's faces! Too much cat piss in all these capitalist political speeches!"

The black politician says: "There is not enough Me-Me-Me-Me in this world! We need more Me-Me-Me-Me! Whether I'm white or black, I want more Me-Me-Me-Me!"

All the black people on stage yell: "More Me-Me-Me-Me for all the politicians & dictators! More armaments and blam-blam-blam and tat-tat-tat to save the world for democracy!"

And the white politician says: "Lots of extraterrestrial doo-doo is on the horizon! Extraterrestrial doo-doo is in the future! Our future is bright with extraterrestrial doo-doo!"

And all the white people yell: "A future of postmodern architecture soaring out of extraterrestrial buttholes! A future of lots & lots of extraterrestrial doo-doo for everybody!"

And the black politician says: "I love it when a black woman sits on a white boy's face! I want black women sitting on white boys' faces for everybody!"

And all the black people yell: "Black women sitting on white boys' faces for everybody!"

And then suddenly everyone freezes. All is quiet...

The transsexual says sarcastically: "Voom-voom-voom for me! Lots of toads jumping around your brains for you! Extraterrestrial Pussy for everybody!"

And then the rich bourgeois pig comes out on stage and starts throwing money at the white politician & the black politician. And all the supporters of the politicians cheer & cheer as they leave the stage. And the entire orchestra plays Lots of corrupt Jackasses & elephants jumping out of the buttholes of dogs & cats...

And now the only people remaining on stage are the two men, the woman, & the transsexual.

The woman says: "I have a vision of all the world's billionaires in the toilet after I have taken a number two!"

The first man says: "Visions of talking tomatoes bouncing around the supermarket! Visions of Thousands of flying saucers flying out of the Old Testament of the Bible!"

The second man says: "Throw me in a dungeon of pain & pleasure! Throw me in bed with my two daughters so we can make babies just like in the Old Testament!"

And the transsexual announces: "Everybody must Jump in the frying pan right now! Because the hungry cannibals are coming! We must be prepared for zombie religious fanatics flying around on their broomsticks!"

And then the entire symphony orchestra starts playing the invasion of zombie religious fanatics conquering the New World.

And the announcer says: "And now the great dictator of the nation of whatever has arrived to bless us with his oratory. You better clap & sing & shout & cheer or he will have you lined up against the wall and shot."

And with much pomp & ceremony the great dictator marches on stage with a giant crowd of "supporters".

And the grand dictator says: "When I'm sitting on the toilet I think of Salvador Dali eating Greek philosophy! Whenever I scratch my balls I'm thinking of Jesus Christ! And whenever I let a prostitute pee on me I'm thinking of the clouds in the sky walking through my windows...!"

The crowd shouts: "We love you because we don't want to be lined up and shot!"

And the dictator says: "As your dictator I order everybody to MEOW like a thousand cats! As the beloved father of the nation I want To chop off all your arms & legs & ears! And since all the citizens of this great nation are my children, I want all my children to go to Satan school and learn how to be worshipers of evil & lust & sin!"

The crowd shouts: "We adore you because we don't want to be lined up and shot!"

And the dictator says: "Our nation must become a Fantasy! Our nation will be a fantasy in theory, and a nightmare in reality! Under my leadership all nightmares are possible! And speaking of any reality is now forbidden! Reality will never stand in our way!"

The crowd shouts: "We submit to you because we don't want to be lined up and shot!"

And then everything stops. Everybody freezes. There is silence.

And the transsexual says: "I have an empire of wonderful vibrators! I have conquered all the dreams floating around the night! And now all the sexual fantasies of paradise will be mine!"

And then the entire symphony orchestra plays some Little kittens conquering the universe. And the dictator and his supporters leave the stage.

And the first man says: "I was in the 14th century once!"

And the second man says: "I was also there, but I was eaten by a thousand hungry priests bearing the Catholic rituals of cannibalism!"

And the woman says: "You're so lucky! I can't get anybody to eat my Pussy!"

And the transsexual says: "Eat my Pussy! Eat my Pussy! Eat my Pussy!"

And then the woman asks: "Can you talk to the Empress of Eating Pussy, and get her to eat my Pussy?"

That's when the entire orchestra starts playing a Pussy eating contest. And then a preacher walks out on stage. Walking behind him are lots of religious devotees.

The preacher preaches: "The Lord commands you to eat Pussy! Eating Pussy is the way to salvation! And you must give me 10% of the Pussy juices!"

And the devotees shout: "Eat that Pussy with lots of Machiavellian strategy!"

And the preacher preaches: "Eat that Pussy both night & day! Eat that Pussy with lots of religious devotion! Do a service to God and eat that Pussy!"

And the devotees shout: "Glory hallelujah to eating that Pussy!"

And the preacher preaches: "When you eat that Pussy, God is watching with heavenly bliss! Eating Pussy will send you to Pussy eating heaven! The angels sing the praises of Satan when you eat that Pussy!"

And the devotees shout: "We love to eat Pussy!"

And the preacher preaches: "Eating Pussy will open up a universe of thousands of galaxies to you! The Lord will conquer the Earth with Pussy eating! Jesus Christ will cum again with lots of Pussy eating! And Jesus Christ will eat everybody's Pussy!"

And all the devotees start throwing money at the preacher.

And then the whole orchestra starts playing a Pussy eating kingdom of God. And the preacher and his devotees walk off the stage...

And then the transsexual asks: "What tunnel of wonder & joy is a Pussy?"

And the first man asks: "Is Pussy a choo-choo train traveling off to the exotic lands of the bedroom?"

And the woman asks: "Is my Pussy a desert of Israel, or a flood of Noah, or both?"

And the second man asks: "Which is the way to Pussy?"

And then the organ starts to play the way to Pussy. And a priest with his congregation walks on stage...

And the priest sings in a Gregorian chant: "Eat the virgin Mary's Pussy! Eat the Virgin Mary's Pussy with lots of ketchup & mustard & relish! Eat the Virgin Mary's Pussy with so much thunder & lightning!"

And the transsexual shouts out: "Amen!"

And the priest sings in the Gregorian chant: "Eating Pussy is so good for the blue sky! Heavenly things cum from eating Pussy! So Much rainbows & sunrises & sunsets from eating Pussy!"

And meanwhile in front of the stage the first man has started performing oral sex on the second man...

And the transsexual shouts out: "Amen!"

And the priest sings in a Gregorian chant: "Everyone must eat Pussy to go to heaven! Heaven is filled with heavenly Pussy eating! Thou shall eat Pussy with lots of Jesus dying on the cross! Thou shall eat Pussy with lots of blessing from the Pope! Thou shall eat Pussy with lots of poetry!"

And meanwhile the woman has started to perform oral sex on the priest.

And the entire congregation shouts out: "Amen!"

And then the organ starts playing a giant Pussy in the sky being eaten by all the little devils of hell. And the priest and his congregation leave the stage...

The woman brushing off the semen from the side of her mouth says: "The priest's cum tastes like a Poet jumping off the moon at midnight!"

The first man, also brushing semen from the side of his mouth, says: "Semen tastes like one of Jackson Pollock's paintings! Tasting that semen is like tasting ancient Greek philosophy! Glory hallelujah to tasting semen!"

The transsexual starts to sing: "Eat that cum! Eating that cum is like finding nirvana in the Balzac of the Dalai Lama! Eating cum is the greatest psychedelic revolution ever!"

And then the orchestra starts to play Loads & loads of cum. And while the orchestra plays, a black man is running on stage away from four black cops who are beating up the black man. And while the four black cops beat up the black man, a black nationalist is giving a speech to a bunch of black people on stage.

The black nationalist: "These four black cops beating up a black man is black power! And whose fault is this? It's the fault of the working class white man waiting at the bus stop to get to his job That pays peanuts! Because the working class white man is privileged with peanuts on payday! So, behold this black power, brothers and sisters! Before, four white cops would beat up a black man! I'll tell you brothers and sisters, progress is being made! Black power! Black power! Black power!"

And as the four cops beat up the black man, the four black cops repeat: "Black power! Black power! Black power!"

And then a white female cop Walks up on stage with a gun, and points it at the black man, and shoots him to death while she repeats: "Taser! Taser! Taser!"

And the white female cop faces everybody and says: "That's the power of sisterhood!"

And then the orchestra plays lots & lots of rabbit holes going everywhere... And everybody leaves the stage.

The transsexual sings: "I love sucking the cock of the American President as the band plays 'Hail-to-the-Chief'! I love great homoerotic operas between rival armies on the battlefield! And I love creating giant homoerotic sculptures of the wonderful 1970s!"

The lady asks: "Do you love The beautiful satanic calligraphy that shoots out of your penis into a man's butthole?"

And then the orchestra plays Out-of-control Wing bats doing out-of-control hallucinatory rituals with out-of-control ladies...

And the narrator says over the loudspeaker: "Ladies and gentlemen! The Grand Wizard of the Ku Klux Kockroaches shall honor us with a speech!"

And the Grand Wizard in white robes wearing the mask of a cockroach and the tentacles of a cockroach walks onto the stage, followed by an admiring crowd of human cockroaches all dressed up as the Ku Klux Kockroaches. They all are wearing Klan robes, and they all are wearing cockroach masks, and have the tentacles of cockroaches protruding from their Klan robes.

And the Grand Wizard of the Ku Klux Kockroaches says: "I love to dance like Kubla Khan in a pleasure dome while I'm wearing women's intimate clothing! I love big Black Kock in the beautiful essence of my butthole! Give me more big black Kock!"

And all the Ku Klux Kockroaches on stage cheer wildly.

And the Grand Wizard of the Ku Klux Kockroaches says: "Big black Kock is so Sunny day with lots of blue sky in your heart! Big black Kock is the greatest paintbrush ever! Big black Kock is creating lots of angels singing to you from the ceiling! Three cheers for big Black Cock!"

More cheers from the Ku Klux Kockroaches.

And the Grand Wizard says: "Big black Cock is as wonderful as A black Uncle Sam jizzying Fourth-of-July fireworks everywhere! Let's all celebrate with big black Kock! Glory hallelujah to big black Kock!"

More cheers.

And then the Grand Wizard says: "Let's celebrate big black Kok with lots of immaculate conception! White power & big black Kock together forever! Let's all pledge allegiance together to the Big black Kock of Uncle Sam!"

And then the orchestra plays The Symphony of Big Black Kok. And the Grand Wizard followed by the Ku Klux Kockroaches leave the stage...

And the narrator says over the loudspeaker: "All rise to honor the Honorable Judge Mother Fooker!"

And the Honorable Judge Mother Fokker walks on stage.

And then the judge says: "In the case of Big Corporate Cock Up Your Ass versus The Little Guy I pronounce my judgment in favor of the Big Corporate Cock Up Your Ass!"

And then the bourgeois pig rushes up on stage and throws a bunch of money at the judge.

The judge goes on to say: "Our society is based on worms & fairytales & bomb the fuck Out of all them countries! Without Santa Claus our civilization would collapse! Law & order with lots of Santa Claus is wonderful for all the herpes of our economy!"

As he talks the transsexual, the two
men, & the woman are dancing to the
judge talking...

And the judge says: "Our laws are based
on penguins swimming through phrases
of poetry! Our great nation was founded
on bubblegum & butt fucking & lots &
lots of dildos! And our government needs
lots of dildos to safeguard its citizens!"

And everybody continues dancing to the
judge talking, and then everybody
continues dancing as the orchestra starts
playing law & order with lots of
bubblegum & more bubblegum & more
bubblegum, and the judge starts dancing
off the stage...

www.ingramcontent.com/pod-product-compliance
Lightning Source LLC
LaVergne TN
LVHW051759080426
835511LV00018B/3360